USING MAKERSPACES
FOR SCHOOL PROJECTS™

10 GREAT MAKERSPACE PROJECTS USING

LANGUAGE ARTS

ANITA LOUISE MCCORMICK

Rosen YA

New York

Published in 2018 by The Rosen Publishing Group, Inc.
29 East 21st Street, New York, NY 10010

Library of Congress Cataloging-in-Publication Data

Names: McCormick, Anita Louise, author.
Title: 10 great makerspace projects using language arts / Anita Louise McCormick.
Description: New York : Rosen Publishing, 2018. | Series: Using makerspaces for school projects | Includes bibliographical references and index. | Audience: Grades 6–12.
Identifiers: LCCN 2017002531 | ISBN 9781499438444 (library-bound)
Subjects: LCSH: Makerspaces—Juvenile literature. | Handicraft—Juvenile literature.
Classification: LCC TS171.57 .M33 2018 | DDC 372.5/5044—dc23
LC record available at https://lccn.loc.gov/2017002531

Manufactured in the United States of America

CONTENTS

INTROD

Maker Faires are conventions where makers of all kinds can get together and share ideas about projects that interest them.

The world you are about to enter is a world of ideas made real. Not just the ideas and imagination of one person, but the imaginations of many. It is a world created by writers, artists, and designers. People who know how to make props, film videos, and create circuits and computer programs also live here. It is a world where robotic devices can be set to act out stories, too.

Welcome to the world of makerspaces!

Makerspaces are places where people can come together and tinker with ideas and projects that fascinate them. Becoming part of makerspace groups has advantages over working on your own. Most makerspaces have relaxed, cooperative environments. You can learn from each other and brainstorm. If something doesn't work and you need help, you can ask other members for advice. If something doesn't work, it only means to try a another approach.

Once makers have created something, they often want to connect with other people that enjoy the same challenges. Some do this in local meet-up groups. Others write blogs and create videos to share their discoveries. There are many popular podcasts and YouTube channels for people who are interested in making. *Make:* magazine and other websites offer opportunities for makers of all sorts to submit their projects for review and possible publication.

Maker Faires are events where makers come to see what other makers have been doing. They are sometimes billed as The Greatest Show (And Tell) On Earth. As the maker movement becomes more popular, such events are springing up all over the world. They allow makers of all sorts to get together, talk about what they have learned through the process of making, and display their work. Some Maker Faires are mostly for people working with computers, robotics, and highly technical experiments. Other Maker Faires are geared more toward crafters of fiber, wood, or other low-tech materials.

Maker Faires may attract participants that want to create new ways to tell and illustrate stories. One exhibit at the 2016 Maker Faire was entitled "Fairy Tales, Science Fiction and Freud, Telling Stories." This project was a collaboration of artists Marianne Petit and Jody Culkin. In this exhibit of their work, Petit and Culkin found ways to combine art and technology with nineteenth-century science and science fiction to tell stories in an entirely new way. The books they chose to illustrate were *Interpretation of Dreams* by Sigmund Freud and stories from *Der Struwwelpeter*, an early children's book written by German author Heinrich Hoffman.

Their exhibit included elaborately designed pop-up books that featured original art to illustrate these stories from the past. Other stories were illustrated with animated art, and displayed, along with a musical track, on LED computer screens. Still other stories had cut out drawings attached to solid bases. Through many different approaches to storytelling, Petit and Culkin helped to show how the world of makerspaces and literature could come together and enhance each other in entirely new ways.

CHAPTER ONE

MEET THE MAKERSPACE

Imagine you had a place where you could experiment on any project that interests you. A place where everything from computers, tools, electronic parts, and robotic modules were available for your use. Cardboard, cloth, scissors, and a sewing machine, and all sorts of gadgets may also be available. Other students would be using the space as well—some working on individual projects, others working in groups. If you needed help with a project, you could ask other students or teachers for help.

Sound like fun? That is exactly what is happening in makerspaces in schools, libraries, and community centers all over the world.

Many kinds of projects can happen in makerspaces. While some focus solely on computer science and technology such as 3D printers and robotics, others are more broad based. They include places for users to engage in other kinds of making, such as wood work, metal work, art, crafts, and sewing.

FROM STEM TO STEAM

Nearly everyone knows how makerspace activities can help make STEM (science, technology, engineering, and math) classes more interesting and bring real-world applications to theories taught in class. Students who are interested in sci-

While sewing machines may not be as high tech as computers, 3D printers, and robots, they are still useful pieces of equipment in many makerspaces.

ence, engineering, math, and computers have been part of makerspaces since the beginning.

But now some schools are finding ways to bring makerspace ideas and technology to other classes, including the arts. When arts, including language arts, are added to STEM programs, they are known as STEAM programs.

Even antique writing tools, such as a quill pen, ink, and paper, can be used for making projects in a STEAM language arts class.

While STEAM is a newer concept to most educators than STEM programs, they are growing in popularity as school administrators learn how much they can add to the learning experience.

MAKING MAKERSPACES WORK IN SCHOOLS

At one time, the only places students made things in school were in art class, shop, and sewing classes. Usually, all the equipment needed for the projects was kept in that classroom. But now that makerspaces, with their wide variety of making supplies, are becoming more popular, school administrators must decide where to locate makerspaces so that students have access to the workspace and equipment.

While some schools have makerspaces in science classrooms or computer rooms, other schools have built makerspaces in common areas, such as libraries.

Scheduling can also be an issue. Most makerspaces are not large enough for all the students who might want to use the space at one time, even when there are multiple work stations. Some school administrators open makerspaces before school, during lunch, after school, and even on weekends to give students more time to experiment.

Many STEM makerspace activities involve circuits, computers, math, and robotics. But STEAM makerspaces incorporate the fields of art and literature. This means that in addition to the technology often associated with STEM makerspaces, sewing machines, cardboard, wood, paint, markers, and other lower-tech ways of making are also available to participants.

TECHNOLOGY AND COMMUNICATION

Makerspace activities in language arts class might seem strange at first, but they actually fit right in! The process of making, in one way or another, has always played an important role in language arts and communication. Before books could be read, they had to be printed, or "made." Stage plays are the result of many hours of not only writing, but costume, set, and stage design. Many kinds of making and communications technology must be employed for radio and TV broadcasts to reach their audience.

Think of the technology that goes into the computers we use to read and write on. And what about the video and special effects that go into producing TV shows and movies? Now you have a better understanding of how computers, robotics, and other technical knowledge can play vital roles in bringing stories alive for a worldwide audience. Does this sound interesting? Can't wait to get started? Great!

For thousands of years, dressing up in costumes and acting out plays has been a popular way of telling stories throughout the world.

Whatever kind of maker you are and whatever materials you like to use, there is a place for you in the wonderful world of makerspaces! Even if you have little to no technical knowledge, these ten projects will help you find ways of bringing the innovative ideas of makerspace culture into your language arts class.

CHAPTER TWO

Starting with the Basics

Do you want to get started with making but you don't know where to start?

Perhaps your school does not have a dedicated makerspace area. Still, you can start making projects for your language arts class with everyday materials you probably already have at home and school. Making does not have to be expensive or complicated. Scissors, paper, cardboard, markers, paint, and glue are easy and inexpensive to obtain. They can be used as creative materials for many exciting projects.

Since kindergarten, most of us have been creating with these basic materials. They can be used for drawing, building, designing, and cutting. They can be used to tell stories we already know, or to experiment with different ways of presenting new stories and ideas. Until the digital age, nearly every author and artist wrote or sketched out their stories with paper and marking materials.

So let's get started and see what you can create!

PROJECT 1: TIME PORTAL

Time portals are not just for science fiction. Every story you read transports you to a time and place that is different from your own.

GETTING CREATIVE WITH CARDBOARD

Cardboard is more than something that's used for making boxes. With a little imagination and some tape, markers, and paint, cardboard can be turned into just about anything! On top of that, it's usually inexpensive or free.

Cardboard is not just something for little kids to play with. One person who knows this is professional artist and curator, Lori Zimmer. She's

(continued on the next page)

Cardboard is one of the easiest construction materials to obtain, and its use is limited only by your imagination.

(continued from the previous page)

the author of *The Art of Cardboard, Big Ideas for Creativity, Collaboration, Storytelling and Reuse*, which shows amazing sculptures and other works of art that can be created using cardboard as a primary material. She enjoys promoting the idea of using materials that might otherwise end up in landfills. She also says that pieces of art made from cardboard and other recycled items should be considered just as valid as art made from expensive store bought materials.

Cardboard is a great material for exploring your creativity. Every year, the nonprofit organization Imagination Foundation hosts the Global Cardboard Challenge. It's designed to encourage students to experiment and see what they can make out of cardboard. Projects include cosplay costumes, doll houses, puppet theaters, and devices with moving parts, such as space ships. In 2016, the fifth year of the event, the Cardboard Challenge attracted over 98,000 participants from around the world. They worked in schools, libraries, and community center makerspaces. Some were home-schooled students. The results were amazing and as varied as the imaginations of the participants.

For your project, imagine that you have traveled from the present to the time or setting of a book you recently read. Now think about how you might want to represent the trip. Create the time portal from materials you have available or can easily acquire. Once it is finished, give a presentation about why you chose the items you used to construct it.

For example, if you decided on a book from the Harry Potter series, what items would you use to take you into the magical world that Harry Potter inhabits? Make a list of items you might want to replicate as part of your time portal. Magic hats and wands? Capes? An owl? A broom? The scenery of the time and place where Harry lived? These items can be drawn, painted, or glued to your time portal. The structure of the time portal itself can be something that represents both our timeline and the world of Harry Potter.

Alternatively, you might want to make the time portal an object that might not be too noticeable in its surroundings, such as the phone booth shaped Tardis Dr. Who uses it to travel through time and space. Or it could be a device that is unlike anything on Earth. Another example is the gateway used in the movie and TV series *Stargate* to travel to other planets. In the show, the gateway comes from an extraterrestrial civilization. If you decide to take that approach, you will still want to decorate your time portal with items that represent the time and place you want to connect with.

HOW TO PROCEED

1. Select a novel or short story for your project. It should be something everyone in the group has read or has time to read before starting.

2. Make a list of the items or ideas you want to represent. After you brainstorm about this, discuss which are the best to use, and how you want to represent them in your time portal.

3. Decide on a structure for your time portal. Are you making a cardboard structure large enough to actually walk

Since the Harry Potter books and movies became popular, they have inspired many fans to create fan fiction, art, costumes, wands, wizard hats, and other props.

through, or something smaller? If your time and space is limited, you can even use a piece of paper to draw your time portal and the items or ideas you want to incorporate into the project.

4. Design and build the time portal. If you think of new ideas in the process, it's fine to add them in.

5. Explain your time portal to the class and discuss how and why you made it. Tell them about things you learned while experimenting, and if the project gave you new ideas about the story that inspired it.

PROJECT 2: GRAPHIC LIT

Graphic novels are everywhere these days. They range from science fiction, detective stories, steampunk, and even alternate histories. Some nonfiction books are also written and illustrated as graphic novels. The illustrations in graphic novels can be drawn in comic book style or art made from photos that were digitally edited to look like drawings.

THINGS YOU'LL NEED

- A story to illustrate
- Paper, pens, paint or other marking supplies
- Or, alternatively, a computer or iPad® with art software or apps

HOW TO PROCEED

1. Think of a story that would make a great graphic novel. Or maybe you would like to create your own story.

Most software programs designed for creating comics include a variety of speech bubbles that will add interest and excitement to your comic strip or graphic novel.

2. Pick a scene from the story that you can illustrate in several panels.

3. Brainstorm about how you might represent the characters and the world they live in.

4. If you are doing this as a group project, one person can be in charge of designing the storyboard, which shows where text and illustrations are placed. Someone else can do the actual drawing. Another person can do the lettering. If you want, you can do this project as a mixed media collage by using images from magazines and newspapers, or printed images from the internet.

5. When you have completed your graphic novel, present it to the class for comments. Jot down the class's feedback.

6. Afterward, consider your work. Did doing this project give you more insights on the story? How did the project make you feel about the possibility of creating a full length graphic novel some day? Write a short essay answering these questions and reflecting on the comments that the class made about your project. When you are finished, turn the essay in to your teacher.

CHAPTER THREE

SEWING MACHINES IN THE DIGITAL AGE

When you think of makerspaces, you may picture people experimenting with coding, circuits, and robotics. But sewing machines can also play an important role in designing and assembling makerspace projects. This is especially true now that most sewing machines are highly computerized and can accomplish tasks that few in the past could have imagined.

Until recently, sewing machines were used mostly for sewing clothes, quilts, and craft projects. Most machines could handle only light to medium-weight fabric, and had a limited variety of stitches. But in the last few decades, sewing machines have come a long way. Most modern sewing machines are highly computerized and can sew a wide variety of fancy embroidery stitches. Because of this, sewing machines are not only being used to hold pieces of fabric together, but to decorate them as well.

SEWING CIRCUITS INTO FABRIC

In today's makerspaces, sewing machines are being used to sew electronic circuits into clothing. They are also used to create works of electronic fiber art and repurpose items that might otherwise have been tossed into the landfill. Special

High-tech sewing machines, such as the one in this photo, can be used not only to sew pieces of fabric together, but also to embroider or add other decoration to cloth projects.

conductive thread can be used not only to sew wired circuits into fabric, but also to create circuits from the thread itself. This has led to many "soft-circuit" creations. Examples are cloth bracelets with LED lights and jewelry and clothing that plays music, lights up, or does other amazing things. The possibilities are endless.

While many sewing machines are strictly for use with fabric, industrial-grade sewing machines that can stitch together heavier materials are available in some makerspaces. So it's a good idea to learn as much as you can about the sewing machine you have access to before planning your sewing-related makerspace projects.

COSTUMES FOR COSPLAY AND DRAMA CLASS

Sewing machines are especially useful for language arts projects. They are often used by students who want to create cosplay costumes in makerspaces. They can be used for creating costumes and props for drama class. Some students even use sewing machines to create puppets to act out stories in language arts class.

PROJECT 3: COSPLAY LIT

You may think of cosplay as a way to dress up as superheroes, villains, or other characters from modern comics. But cosplay can be used to gain a better understanding of characters from stories who live in any place or era. For this project, pick a story and decide which character everyone in the group would like to cosplay. Then, research the clothing that was commonly worn in that place and during that time. The internet has many websites that can be helpful for planning your costume. Once you have done that, see what materials are available that could be used to construct a cosplay outfit. When your cosplay outfits are complete, you can cosplay a scene from the story for your class.

Steampunk is Made for Makerspaces

Steampunk is a type of science fiction or fantasy movement that is usually set in the 1800s. It often incorporates wildly imaginative steam-powered machinery. Some steampunk stories are set in Victorian-era England. Others are set in American cities or in the American West. They often involve an alternative history, where steam power is used to run computers, time machines, space ships, and other inventions.

The steampunk literary movement started in the 1980s. It was inspired by early science fiction writers such as H. G. Wells, the author of *The Time Machine* and *War of the Worlds*. With the help of the internet, steampunk fans from all over the world started to connect. Since the early 2000s, steampunk has grown from a subgenre of science fiction and fantasy into a fully fledged cultural movement. It includes not only stories and novels, but fashion, music, magazines, and movies. The growing interest in steampunk has led to many societies, meet-ups, conventions, and festivals where fans arrive in steampunk attire. This includes costumes, jewelry, and hats that look like they came out of the 1800s. Often people are fitted with goggles and fancy gears and bring machines, too.

(continued on the next page)

(continued from the previous page)

While readymade steampunk costumes and gear can be ordered through specialty stores, many fans enjoy the challenge of making their own costumes, props, and machines. This can add to the steampunk experience and help participants feel like they are actually going back in time to the exciting age of steampunk innovation and invention. While steampunk-related devices are designed to look Victorian, for practical reasons, they are usually powered by electricity. Since the steampunk movement has grown so large, enthusiasts are likely to find people with similar interests who can help them design their projects.

Steampunk costumes are a fun way of experiencing a fantasy world where gears, goggles, and clothing from another century come together to create fun, imaginative gatherings.

THINGS YOU'LL NEED

- Characters from a story to cosplay
- Cloth or ready made pieces of clothing
- Sewing supplies
- Computer, iPad®, or paper for taking notes
- Cardboard, poster paper, or other materials, to design set

HOW TO PROCEED

1. For example, if you were going to cosplay Sherlock Holmes, you would want to look up the way people dressed in the time that his story is set. If the story you read gave information about Sherlock Holmes's appearance and the way he behaved, make sure to write that down. If you are building a set or a background where Sherlock Holmes had his office or went to solve a case, make note of that, too.

2. Once you have done that, brainstorm about what you can do to make your cosplay of Sherlock Holmes as authentic to the character as possible.

3. Ask yourself: are there other characters in the Sherlock Holmes story, such as Watson, you would like to cosplay as well?

4. Figure out what materials do you have to work with. Can you find clothes to modify to better fit your needs? Are there things you might want to borrow from the drama club or a local theater group?

5. After you have discussed these things, plan the costumes you want to make. If they are close fitting, find articles of clothing you can trace around to make a pattern.

6. After you have created the costumes, try cosplaying the characters.

7. Then, journal about your experience. What did you learn about Sherlock Holmes or the character you played, that you did not know before? How do you think it might have felt for you to live in that time period?

8. Once you have your ideas together, write a blog or make a video about your experience to share with the class or post online.

PROJECT 4: LITERARY WALL HANGING

Many of us have seen memory quilts, or wall hangings, people make by sewing together hand-decorated fabric squares. These special wall hangings are often made to honor birthdays, anniversaries, weddings, or other life events. Sometimes, they are made as a gift for a family that is moving out of the area as a special way to remember their friends.

In the same way, you can create a literary wall hanging by decorating squares in a way that tells something about your favorite book.

A literary wall hanging can create a lasting memory of your reading experience for the year. When the school year is over, it would make a nice gift for your language arts teacher.

THINGS YOU'LL NEED

- Cloth
- Scissors

Fabric paint or fabric markers
Thread to embroider and sew
the quilt together
Hand sewing needles
Sewing machine (if you do
not have a sewing machine
available, the wall hanging can
be sewn by hand, or it can be
stapled or tied together)
Dowel or broom handle (op-
tional)

HOW TO PROCEED

Cut pieces of cloth into
twelve-inch squares, and give a
square to everyone that wants
to participate. Each person can
decorate the square to represent a book they enjoy. The
squares can be decorated with
fabric markers, paint, embroidery, machine sewing, or
whatever else you want.

Once the squares have all been
created and the paint is dry, find an
area where you can lay the squares
out as you decide how you want to
organize them. If you do not have

By cutting images from several
pieces of cloth, sewing them
together, and decorating them
with stitches and paint, you
can create a cloth representa-
tion of a scene from a story.

29

enough decorated squares to finish some rows, blank fabric squares can be added to fill in the space.

The next step is to attach the squares together. You can accomplish that with a sewing machine, hand sewing, a stapler, or by threading a large needle with yarn or embroidery floss and using it to tie the squares together.

When the wall hanging has been assembled, you will want to display it for everyone to see. If you want, you can sew loops on the top of the piece and hang it on a dowel, broom handle, and so on. Or, you can use thumb tacks to attach it to the wall.

CHAPTER FOUR

VIDEO CAMERAS AND EDITING SOFTWARE

Today, video cameras are everywhere! In addition to cameras purposely built to record videos, nearly all smartphones and digital cameras on the market today are capable of recording video. Most devices that record video come with software that allows you to do basic video editing. This, combined with the worldwide connectivity of the internet, makes video a great tool for communicating images and ideas.

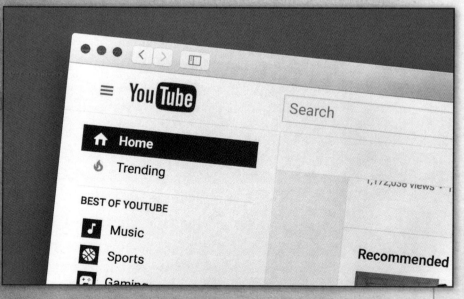

YouTube is one of the most popular video-sharing websites on the internet. It gives everyone with a video camera the opportunity to reach a worldwide audience.

The Hillywood Show—the Power of Cosplay and YouTube

Do you love to dress up as your favorite characters and cosplay? Hilly and Hannah Hindi, stars of *The Hillywood Show*, do! In fact, the Hindi sisters enjoy cosplay so much that they built a YouTube empire from their knack for making entertaining parody videos of their favorite TV shows and movies.

Hilly and Hannah received their first recognition in 2006 when they won third place in an AOL video contest. With the encouragement and support of their parents and friends, they went on to create more videos. These include highly entertaining parodies of popular movies and TV shows such as *Dr. Who*, *Lord of the Rings*, *Harry Potter*, *The Hunger Games*, *The Walking Dead*, and *Twilight*. Some of their video parodies have millions of views on YouTube.

As Hilly and Hannah progressed and learned more about the craft of creating video parodies, the costumes and sets became more elaborate, and dance numbers were included. By the time Hilly and Hannah decided to create a parody of *Supernatural* in 2015, their YouTube channel had become so popular that cast members of the show even asked to be part of the video.

Besides having fun with their own unique version of cosplay, the Hindi sisters have found a way to make income from living out their passion. In addition to selling *The Hillywood Show* merchandise on their website and making money from YouTube ads, they set up a Patreon account. There, fans can pledge monthly donations to help cover the expenses of producing their parodies. At the time of writing this, *The Hillywood Show*'s Patreon account brought in over $11,000 a month from an international audience.

EDITING YOUR VIDEOS

Many free or inexpensive video-editing computer programs and apps make video editing an easy process. These include YouTube Capture, Windows Movie Maker, Apple iMovie, Blender, Filmora, and Lightworks. You do not need fancy equipment to create video presentations people will want to watch. YouTube, Facebook, and many other sites are filled with examples of what is possible with home and school video.

PROJECT 5: MAKE A BOOK TRAILER

You have probably seen movie trailers, but how about book trailers? Video book trailers are often created by authors or publishers. They show the public what the book is about, and why they might enjoy reading it. With the video editing and recording equipment available today, you can create your own book trailers, too.

WHAT YOU'LL NEED

- Any device that records video and audio
- A video editing program
- Paper for creating a storyboard
- Computer or iPad®
- Connection to the internet

HOW TO PROCEED

First, select a book you want to make a trailer about. Then, decide how you want to present it. For example, let's say your group decides to create a book trailer about the historical novel, *Number the Stars* by Lois Lowry. Then, the book trailer would communicate something about what the main character Annamarie Johansen's life was like in Copenhagen during World War II and the hardships her family had to face on a daily basis. Next, you would tell how things became much more challenging when Annamarie found out that the Nazis planned to send the Jews in Denmark to death camps. Along with the help of the Danish resistance group, she found the courage to help save the life of her best friend, Ellen Rosen, from the Nazis.

The book trailer you create can include spoken word, text, art, photographs, and videos. You can write a script or start a storyboard by using sticky notes. Then, when you decide what you want to include, write and draw it on paper. A storyboard is a way of drawing out boxes to represent the scenes in your production on paper before you start. You can also create the storyboard by using software on your computer if you want.

When you plan a book trailer, make sure to tell enough about the book to interest readers, but not give away the ending.

If you need ideas, many book trailers created by students can be found on YouTube and educational websites, such as schooltube.com and booktrailersforreaders.com.

Lois Lowry is the author of *Number the Stars*. She has written more than thirty books and won two Newbery Medals for her work.

COPYRIGHT LAWS—WHAT YOU CAN AND CAN'T USE

If you plan to publish your book trailer on the internet, it is important that you understand what you can legally use without violating copyright laws. Fair use is an important term to know. It refers to the amount of copyright work you can use without having to get permission from the creator of the work or their publisher. What is fair use depends on the length of the piece you are quoting from, how much of the work you intend to quote, and what you plan to use it for.

Quoting just a few sentences from a book for school assignments and other educational projects is usually okay, but if you talk about the story in your own words instead of quoting material from the book, you should not have to worry about copyright infringement.

Also, if you use your own art, video, and photographs to share your impressions of the story, you are safer than using art and photos from the book. Plus, it's more fun to be creative and use your own words and images to let people know why you like the book and what makes it so special!

For more information on copyright laws, check the US Copyright Office website, or the website of the copyright office of the country you live in.

PROJECT 6: "LIVE FROM THE SCENE" VIDEO REPORT

Imagine you are at the scene of a fictional story or real event you have recently read about. If you were a TV news reporter, how would you present this scene to the public?

Modern video cameras and computer technology now make it possible to record interviews from nearly any location and share them on the internet.

In your report, you can record and show video, and interview students acting out the part of witnesses, neighbors, political figures, and experts. If weather was a factor in the story, you can bring on a student acting as a meteorologist to explain how weather was a contributing factor in the event.

WHAT YOU'LL NEED

- Any device that records video and audio
- Computer, tablet, or iPad®
- An editing program
- Props and costumes
- Backdrop
- Connection to the internet

HOW TO PROCEED

For example, perhaps you have read *Freedom Train: The Story of Harriet Tubman,* by Dorothy Sterling. You might want to make a "live from the scene" video about how Harriet Tubman helped a group of slaves escape bondage. You could have your reporter interviewing a person portraying Harriet Tubman and the people she helped. The student portraying the reporter could ask them about their experiences as slaves. They could also ask them to talk about some of the things they experienced on their journey to freedom.

If you have time, create a background, or backdrop for your video. You can use cardboard, a roll of bulletin board paper, or even film the video outdoors.

When you have made and edited your video, show it to other students that have read the same book and see if they have feedback or additional suggestions. If you decide to change something, you can go back and reedit it with your video editing software.

Once you are finished, you might want to post your video on YouTube or another video-hosting website so others can enjoy your work!

CHAPTER FIVE

3D PRINTERS MAKE IDEAS REAL

Did you ever wish you could come up with an idea, then see it appear in three dimensions? If you have access to a 3D printer and understand how to use modeling software, that wish can become a reality.

A 3D printer makes it possible to design and create in ways that were never before possible. They take digital

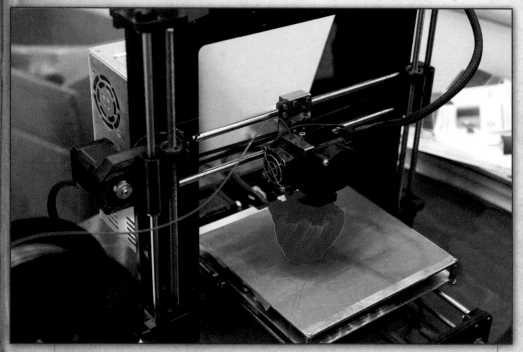

Makerspaces equipped with 3D printers have the advantage of being able to print objects that might not otherwise be available for their projects.

information you provide from a computer file and transform it into objects you can hold in your hand. When 3D printers first came out, they were used mostly by scientists, engineers, and for industrial use. But as prices continue to fall, they are now becoming a standard piece of equipment in more and more makerspaces.

SOFTWARE FOR 3D PRINTING

Before you print something with a 3D printer, you will need to create a model of it on your computer. You can create these models by using software that takes the instructions you provide and translates it into a language that a 3D printer can understand. This then translates your wishes into a 3D-printed item. This type of software is known as CAD, meaning computer-aided design. It is also called modeling software, because when you use it, you are creating a model of the item you want to print on the computer screen.

Two popular brands of free modeling software to use for 3D-printer projects are Blender and Sketch-up. Both programs have many features that can help you use your computer to bring ideas from your imagination into 3D reality.

If you don't have time to design 3D-printable objects from scratch, there's a solution. Numerous websites offer downloadable files for predesigned items you can print as they are or modify to your own specifications. Some of the more popular websites for 3D-printable designs are Thingiverse, Sketchfab, CG Trader, and MyMiniFactory. Thingiverse is operated by MakerBot Industries and hosts

3D Printers Move from Science Labs into Schools and Homes

As 3D-printer technology developed, the prices for basic 3D printers fell to the point that people outside science labs and businesses could afford them. The earliest affordable printers that made their way into schools and homes were slow and could be a challenge to operate. But still, the fascination of making something you designed on a computer come out in 3D made them something many wanted.

The first inexpensive 3D printers were objects of fascination. Initially, the items many people printed were novelties that were created just so they could watch the printers work. They marveled at the process as the 3D printers used spaghetti-like material to transform digital data into objects.

But soon, other applications made owning 3D printers more practical. For example, it was often easier to make a 3D replica of a broken part than to order one and wait for its arrival. In the field of medicine, 3D printers are being used to make artificial limbs that fit better than the standard artificial limbs amputees used in the past. In the world of education, 3D printers are a good way to create models of concepts that could at one time only be shown in two-dimensional illustrations in textbooks.

one of the largest collections of free 3D-printing files on the internet.

Thingiverse has an educational area on their website that features many excellent ideas for using 3D printing for school projects for all ages and classes.

Many of the designs available on 3D-design websites were created by makerspace enthusiasts that want to share their work and give other makers the opportunity to use it and expand on it. Once you have learned how to design for 3D printers, you might want to add your work to their collection for others to enjoy!

PROJECT 7: MAPPING IT OUT

Using CAD software and a 3D printer, create a map of a place you are reading about in a class assignment. Once your map is printed, you can paint it and draw in features. You can make it etched, flat, or 3D topographical. You might want to add LED lights to represent cities and towns on a large-scale map, or homes and businesses on a smaller-scale map. What do you notice about the terrain of the story now that you can see it?

(As an alternative project, you can create maps with a laser cutter. Or you can make maps with clay, papier mâché, or even hand draw and decorate them.)

For example, if you decide to make a 3D map of the region where the novel *Watership Down* by Richard Adams takes place, you might want to go online and explore the region first.

CAD drawing software can be used to visualize your ideas and create a set of digitized instructions a 3D printer can understand.

You can obtain a geographic map of *Watership Down* and the surrounding area in England. This will give you much more information than the ink-drawn map in the novel. Fans of the novel who are familiar with the area have created websites with links to maps that make it easy to see where the warrens, rivers, bridges, farms, and other geographic features are located on Google Maps.

Google Earth's satellite images and ability to show areas from different angles can give you an even better view of the region and simplify the process of 3D printing your map.

HOW TO PROCEED

Download and install the free program Google Earth.

Next, download and install MICRODEM, a free application that's available from the US Naval Academy website at http://www.usna.edu.

Then, download and install the srtm4.1 plugin (or the current version of the program) for Google Earth. Once it is installed, the strm4.1 program can be found in Google Earth under the My Places navigation. Click on the Elevation square and grids will appear on the global image. Locate and click on the square you want to print.

Once you have saved the file you created for the map, use the instructions that came with your digital printer to convert the map into 3D.

After your 3D printer has printed the map, you might want to paint it so it will look more realistic. Besides the information you gained from the instruction here, viewing the images on Google Maps and Google Earth can help you to better understand the landscape features. You might want to drill holes in the map for battery-operated LED lights to show where buildings are or, alternatively, areas where the *Watership Down* rabbits had their nests.

PROJECT 8: AND THE AWARD GOES TO...

Think of a character in a book you read that you'd like to present with an award.

Some things to consider are: Why do you want to give this character an award? What would that award look like? What symbols would you include?

Awards and trophies come in all shapes and sizes. They are a way of honoring accomplishments and showing appreciation for a job well done.

For example, if you read *A Christmas Carol* by Charles Dickens, you might decide to give Ebenezer Scrooge an award for changing his attitude about celebrating Christmas and helping less fortunate people in his community. You might want to design an award for him that reflects the place and time he lived in 19th century England, as well as include representations of the ghosts that visited him. You might also want to include the goose he bought for Bob Cratchit's family as a symbol of his change of heart.

HOW TO PROCEED

Once you have some ideas, draw some sketches and discuss your ideas with others in your group. After you have agreed on ideas for the award you want to make, use CAD software to design it. When you are satisfied with your design, send the file to your 3D printer.

After the award has been printed, you can paint and decorate it, or add other items to it, such as sequins and gold-colored trim. How do you think the person receiving the award would respond?

If you want, you can act out the presentation as part of your class project.

CHAPTER SIX

ROBOTS RULE!

When you watch science fiction movies, do you ever think that you might someday have robotic servants to help with things you'd rather not do? You don't have to wait. Robots are everywhere these days! Any device that preforms an action programmed by humans is considered a robot. This includes smartphones, car starters, coffee makers that come on automatically, and so on. Whenever you use a remote control for an electronic device, you are using a robot.

MAKING YOUR OWN ROBOTS

Many makerspaces include robotics kits that can make designing and programming robots relatively easy. These kits include LEGO Mindstorms, Ozobot, Arduino, and VEX. Using robotics kits is a great way to learn about robotics and experiment with simple coding, or programming.

There are even computer apps, such as The Robot Factory, where by playing a game, you can start to learn the basics of what robots are capable of doing.

Robots have one thing in common. They all need programming to receive their instructions. Otherwise, they would do nothing. Robots receive their instructions through programming code that is sent to their microcontrollers. They then take these instructions and put them into action.

One language used by many new programmers is Scratch. Scratch, a visual programming language developed by MIT

Media Lab, was first released to the public in 2007. Today, over 800,000 people, mostly students, use the Scratch website to experiment with coding, create games, and program robots. LEGO robotics kits, Arduino boards, and numerous other tech products can be controlled through Scratch coding.

Other languages used for programming robotics kits are LEGO NXT-G, LEGO EV3, RobotC, Python, C, and Java. Not all robots can be programmed with the same languages,

School robotics teams and clubs provide great opportunities to learn about robots and what they can do.

though. Some can understand only one language, while others can understand more than one. If your school has robotic kits, you should be able to go online and find out what language or languages they use.

Robotics clubs in schools often host challenges where teams of students are given a problem and their task is to design a robot to solve it. These challenges are fun ways to learn about robots and how to design and program them to accomplish a wide variety of tasks.

PROJECT 9: ROBOT TO THE RESCUE!

What problem in your school or community would you like to see a robot solve? Is it something your read about in a science magazine? Perhaps instead it is an idea you got from watching a documentary or a movie about robots.

HOW TO PROCEED

If your school has a robotics team, brainstorm with them. Then, experiment to create a prototype of this robot.

Once you have your robot, test it to see if it can successfully perform the task. If not, keep trying.

If for some reason it is not possible to design a robot to perform the task at this time, write a story or article about what it would be like to have a robot that can help with this issue.

Think about this project and see if you have more ideas about what robots might be able to do to remedy this situation. Discuss them with your classmates.

ROBOTS COME ALIVE IN FICTION

Since the early years of science fiction, robots have often played crucial roles in stories. They were artificial beings that usually could move, talk, or otherwise communicate with other characters in the story, play, TV show, or movie.

Robots were used in science fiction for many reasons. Sometimes they were helpers for humans. Sometimes they were used to explore worlds with environments hostile to humans. Sometimes robots showed what life might be like many years in the future, when technology had advanced to the point where a walking electronic assistant might take care of our needs. Other times, robots were used to spin tales about what might happen if technology got out of control to the point that robots could become dangerous to humanity.

Robots first started to appear in fiction during the mid-1800s. "The Steam Man of the Prairies," by Edward S. Ellis, published in 1865, told the tale of a teenage boy who created an artificial being to take on adventures. Tik-Tok, a character in L. Frank Baum's children's novel, *The Wizard of Oz*, was an early example of how writers imagined machines that could walk, think, and talk.

(continued on the next page)

(continued from the previous page)

In his novel *The War of the Worlds*, first published in 1898, H. G. Wells wrote about spacecraft from Mars that landed on Earth. These spacecraft soon began to release three-legged fighting machines (robots) to wipe out the human population. The novel was made into a radio play that caused some people to panic when it was first aired on *The Mercury Theater on the Air* by CBS Radio on October 31, 1938. Some believed the events in the story were actually taking place because the story was told in the style of a news report.

The famous science fiction writer Isaac Asimov wrote novels in which robots played important roles. In his novels, Asimov came up with rules for robots about how they would be permitted to interact with living beings. These rules were first presented in *I, Robot*, published in 1942.

PROJECT 10: FUTURE FICTION

Write a story that involves a robot. Ask yourself: what can this robot do that helps or works against the main character, or society in general? How do the robot's ideas and actions move the story along? What does the robot look like?

Think about stories you've read or movies you've seen that involve robots. What kind of a role did that robot play? How did the robot help or hinder the people in the story? What time period does the story take place in, and in what kind of a society? Does it happen on Earth, in space, or on another planet? As you write the story, think about how the robot might look and behave.

Once you have made those decisions, go to your local makerspace. There, design a prototype of the robot. If there is a robotics club at your school, you might want to invite them to help. If you think of anything else you would like for the robot to do, see if there is a way you can add this to the programming.

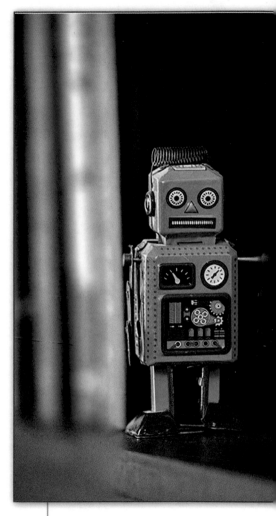

WHAT YOU'LL NEED

- A story or idea that involves a robot
- A robotics kit
- Computer or iPad® to write with
- Video and editing software (if you are making a video as part of the project)
- Connection to the internet

This robot may be small, but with today's technology, it could be capable of amazing things. What do you think it can do?

HOW TO PROCEED

If you are doing this project as a group, you might want to have some people write the story. Others could focus on designing a real robot that can perform the needed action. If you are new to robotics, or just want to explore some ideas, you might want to visit robotic websites. You can also look at books of robotic projects, collaborate with the robotics team at your school, or ask a science or robotics teacher for suggestions.

Alternatively, if you do not have the equipment or knowledge to design a real robot, instead design a costume and have someone cosplay the robot character. If you have time, you might want to create a video about the robot in which you use various backgronds or settings. When you are finished, present the project to the class to see if they have additional suggestions.

If you want, you can write a blog or film a video about how you went about doing this project, the challenges you faced and the things you learned, and post it online.

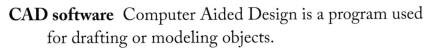

CAD software Computer Aided Design is a program used for drafting or modeling objects.

circuit Path through which electricity flows through wires and components.

coding Writing a set of instructions in a language that computers or robots can understand.

connective thread Metallic thread that can be used to conduct electricity.

cosplay Dressing up and playing the part of a character from books, movies, comic books, or TV shows.

fair use The amount of copyright material you can legally borrow without having to ask permission.

LED A light-emitting diode. A type of light used in many makerspace projects.

parody A song, story, poem, or other creation that is intended as a comical expression of the original piece.

program To write a set of instructions a computer or robot can use to carry out to complete some action.

robot A device that can carry out programmed tasks.

Scratch A system developed at the MIT Media Lab that helps students learn to program interactive stories, games, animations, as well as some kinds of robots.

3D map A map that shows dimensions of the area it replicates.

3D printer A device that can transform information from a digital file into 3D objects.

video editor A software program that allows users to edit video and add music and text.

Canada Youth Robotics Club
2987 West 41st Avenue
Vancouver, BC
Canada
(604) 628-5757
Website: http://www.roboca.org
The Canada Youth Robotics Club is a nonprofit organization
    that focuses on improving robotics education in
    Canadian schools.

Maker Education Initiative
1001 42nd Street, Suite 230
Oakland, CA 94608
Website: http://makered.org
Maker Education Initiative is a nonprofit organization that is
    working with educators and communities to bring about
    makerspace education, especially in underserved areas.

Maker Media, Inc.
1005 Gravenstein Highway N
Sebastopol, CA 95472
Website: http://makermedia.com
Maker Media publishes *Make:* magazine, runs the Makezine
    .com website and organizes numerous Maker Faires.

Scratch
Massachusetts Institute of Technology
77 Massachusetts Avenue
Cambridge, MA 02139

Website: https://scratch.mit.edu
Scratch is a project of the MIT Media Lab to allow people
    to learn to code and share their projects with other code
    enthusiasts online.

STEAM Horizon Awards
Canada Science and Technology Museums Corporation
Foundation
2421 Lancaster Road
Ottawa, ON K1G 5A3
Canada
Website: http://steamhorizonawards.ca
The STEAM Horizon Awards are a project of the Canada
    Science and Technology Museums Corporation
    Foundation and other founding partners. They offer
    scholarships for youth involved with STEAM programs.

WEBSITES

Because of the changing nature of internet links, Rosen Publishing has developed an online list of websites related to the
subject of this book. This site is updated regularly. Please use
this link to access this list:

http://www.rosenlinks.com/UMFSP/language

Blofield, Robert. *How to Make a Movie in 10 Easy Lessons: Learn how to write, direct, and edit your own film without a Hollywood budget.* Lake Forest, CA: Walter Foster Jr, 2015.

Buechley, Leah, and Kanjun Qui. *Sew Electric.* Cambridge, MA: HLT Press, 2013.

Ceceri, Kathy. *Make: Paper Inventions: Machines that Move, Drawings that Light Up, and Wearable Structures You Can Cut, Fold, and Roll.* San Francisco, CA: Maker Media, Inc. 2015.

Ceceri, Kathy. *Making Simple Robots: Exploring Cutting Edge Robotics with Everyday Stuff.* San Francisco, CA: Maker Media, Inc. 2015.

Cohen, Jacob. *Getting the Most Out of Makerspaces to Build Robots,* New York, NY: Rosen Publishing, 2015.

Graves, Colleen and Aaron Graves. *The Big Book of Makerspace Projects: Inspiring Makers to Experiment, Create and Learn.* New York, NY: McGraw-Hill Education, 2016.

Hackett, Chris. *The Big Book of Makerspace Skills: Tools & Techniques for Building Great Tech Projects.* San Francisco, CA: Weldon Owen, 2014.

Heitkamp, Kristina Lyn. *Creating with Digital Sewing Machines.* New York, NY: Rosen Publishing, 2017.

Leavitt, Amie Jane. *Physical Computing and Makerspaces.* New York, NY: Rosen Publishing, 2014.

Maietta, Andrea, and Paolo Aliverti. *The Maker's Manual: A Practical Guide to the New Industrial Revolution.* San Francisco, CA: Maker Media, Inc., 2015.

Petrikowski, Nicki Peter. *Getting the Most Out of Makerspaces to Create with 3D Printers,* New York, NY: Rosen Publishing, 2014.

Roberts, Dustyn. *Making Things Move, DIY Mechanisms for Inventors, Hobbyists, and Artists.* New York, NY: McGraw-Hill Education TAB, 2010.

Salemi, Behnam. *Robot Building for Teens.* Boston, MA: Cengage Learning, PTR, 2014.

Takahara, Miyuu and Kenji Weston. *Cosplay – The Beginner's Masterclass: A Guide To Cosplay Culture & Costume Making: Finding Materials, Planning Ideas, How to Make Clothing, Props & Enjoy Conventions.* CreateSpace, 2015.

Willoughby, Nick. *Making YouTube Videos: Star in Your Own Video!* (Dummies Junior). Hoboken, NJ: For Dummies, 2015.

Zimmer, Lori. *The Art of Cardboard: Big Ideas for Creativity, Collaboration, Storytelling, and Reuse.* Beverly, MA: Rockport Publishers, 2015.

Bradbury, Jeffrey. "Digital Alternatives to Traditional Book Reports." Teachercast. October 1, 2016. http://www .teachercast.net/2016/10/01/digital-alternatives-to -traditional-book-reports/.

Cooper, Jennifer. "Designing a School Makerspace." Edutopia. 2013. September 30, 2013. https://www.edutopia.org /blog/designing-a-school-makerspace-jennifer-cooper.

Creative Educator. "Book Trailers." Retrieved November 7, 2016. http://creativeeducator.tech4learning.com/v07 /lessons/Entice_Your_Reader.

Delaney, Melissa. "Schools Shift from STEM to STEAM." *EdTech* Magazine. April 2, 2014. http://www .edtechmagazine.com/k12/article/2014/04/schools -shift-stem-steam.

DesignSaunders. "TechEducator Podcast: CUE SteamPunk." December 6, 2015. http://designsaunders.com /techeducator-podcast-cue-steampunk.

Elkins, Arlene. "Cosplayers Get Ready for Cons at Artisan's Asylum." Artisan Asylum. August 11, 2016. https:// artisansasylum.com/cosplayers-get-ready-for-cons-at -artisans-asylum.

Hitner, Mara. "3D Printing in Education: Beyond STEM." Matter Hackers. April 29, 2016. https://www .matterhackers.com/articles/3d-printing-in-education -beyond-stem.

Imagination Foundation. "The Global Cardboard Challenge - Just Build It!" Retrieved November 6, 2016. http:// imagination.is/our-projects/cardboard-challenge.

Literature Circles Resource Center. "Story Quilt." Retrieved

November 8, 2016. http://www.litcircles.org/Extension /storyquilt.html.

Maker Faire. "Fairy Tales, Science Fiction, and Freud: Telling Stories." Retrieved November 5, 2016. http://makerfaire .com/maker/entry/58120/.

Own, Lindsey. "Your Students Can Be 'Makers': 16 Projects Invented by Teachers." Getting Smart. June 25, 2015. http://gettingsmart.com/2015/06/your-students-can -be-makers-16-projects-invented-by-teachers/.

PBS Learning Media. "Creating a Hypothesis - The Intelligent Robot." Retrieved November 7, 2016. http:// mpbn.pbslearningmedia.org/resource/ vtl07.la.rv.text .lprobot/creating-a-hypothesis-the-intelligent-robot.

Read Write Think. "Comics and Graphic Novels," Retrieved November 5, 2016. http://www.readwritethink.org /parent-afterschool-resources/activities-projects /comics-graphic-novels-30296.html.

Schwartz, Katrina. "How Robots in English Class Can Spark Empathy and Improve Writing." *KQED* News. July 28, 2016. https://ww2.kqed.org/mindshift/2016/07/28 / how-robots-in-english-class-can-spark-empathy-and -improve-writing/.

Vasko, Stephanie E. "Creating Craftier Engineers: Why students should learn to sew in STEM classes." *Slate*. Retrieved November 5, 2016. http://www.slate.com /articles/technology/future_tense/2015/06/stem_classes _should_include_lessons_about_low_tech_crafts_like _sewing.html.

ABOUT THE AUTHOR

Anita Louise McCormick is a lifelong maker, artist, and writer. She enjoys creating with many different materials. Her mixed media art has been published in *Cloth, Paper, Scissors Magazine* and her paintings are on display in galleries in Maine, where she lives. McCormick is interested in the latest developments in science and technology and is the author of a number of non-fiction books, including *Shortwave Radio Listening for Beginners* and *The Telephone and Telegraph in American History*.

PHOTO CREDITS